LONELY MACHINES

Poems by
Julia Vinograd

Art by Deborah Vinograd

Zeitgeist Press

photo: A. Sienart
Drawings: Deborah Vinograd

ISBN: 0-929730-42-9

Zeitgeist Press
4368 Piedmont Avenue
Oakland CA 94611 U.S.A.

CONTENTS

Blood 1

Ginsberg 2

The Billboard Woman 3

At The Graveyard 4

Lonely Machines 6

Vampires 7

For Eric 8

Rain On The Street 9

For Rosebud And People's Park 10

America 12

Portrait Of A Girl . . . . , , ... 13

Big Trucks 14

The New Depression 15

Scarecrow 16

For Polly, Who Died 18

For Rodney King 19

3 Card Molly 20

Deja Vu 21

After A Street Riot 22

Nut On The Street 25

Hair Wrap 26

Street Sketch 28

Warning 29

Saturday Night 30

The Latest Button 32

The Dark 33

Street Saxophone 34

Street Sketch 35

Bosnia 36

Puppies On The Street 38

For Peter, Who Died 39

Happiness 40

L.A. Burning 41

Street Portrait 42

Mural 43

Boy On A Skateboard 44

Fiddler On The Street 45

Where I Grew Up 46

Too Many Deaths 47

Blues 48

Directions For A Friend Visiting Russia 49

BLOOD
(for Rodney King)

There is a place where blood flows out of the earth
like water rising in a well
or fire from a volcano.
There is a place where blood pours from the earth
and stains everything it touches,
flowing down the aisle at a wedding
and soaking the bride's satin train, thick blood
surrounded by buzzing flies.
Or thru the marble lobbies of condominiums
past the doorman and the flower arrangements,
clotted blood, stinking more than the bum
the doorman turns away.
He can't turn the blood away.
There is a place where blood flows out of the earth
and we look away.
It flows constantly and we build cities
saying "We are strong and the walls are strong,
we can keep it out."
There is a place where blood flows out of the cities,
out of us, and the stronger we are
the faster it flows
and the more it hurts.
A few seconds of film of men beating on a helpless man
and we see that place in the earth
and the blood streams over us, out of us,
dark clotted blood.
We *are* that place in the earth the blood pours out of,
and it never stops, and yes it hurts.
It hurts.

1

GINSBERG

No blame. Anyone who wrote *Howl* and *Kaddish*
earned the right to make any possible mistake
for the rest of his life.
I just wish I hadn't made this mistake with him.
It was during the Vietnam war
and he was giving a great protest reading
in Washington Square Park
and nobody wanted to leave.
So Ginsberg got the idea, "I'm going to shout
'the war is over' as loud as I can," he said
"and all of you run over the city
in different directions
yelling the war is over, shout it in offices,
shops, everywhere and when enough people
believe the war is over,
why, not even the politicians
will be able to keep it going."
I thought it was a great idea at the time,
a truly poetic idea.
So when Ginsberg yelled I ran down the street
and leaned in the doorway
of the sort of respectable down on its luck cafeteria
where librarians and minor clerks have lunch
and I yelled "the war is over".
And a little old lady looked up
from her cottage cheese and fruit salad.
She was so ordinary she would have been invisible
except for the terrible light
filling her face as she whispered
"My son. My son is coming home."
I got myself out of there and was sick in some bushes.
That was the first time *I* believed there was a war.

THE BILLBOARD WOMAN

The billboard woman is 20 feet high,
the one lonely men half-hate.
Her high heels alone
are big as a man's head and always black.
The product doesn't matter.
Lights flash on her sign all night
and throw her image into the drivers' eyes.
It would be a mercy if they could crash,
if pieces of flying steel
could slash her paper face
and blood could splatter her gleaming legs.
Her blonde hair hangs over the highway
looking like she'd just climbed out of bed
with someone else.
But it's more than that.
No one can have her, she's 20 feet high
and she was never human.
They didn't use a model, they didn't need one.
They used dreams
the kind lonely men half-hate.
She's watching them now, smiling
the way she watched them
when they thought they were alone.

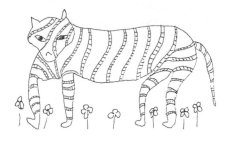

AT THE GRAVEYARD

I saw the old women at the town graveyard.
They'd all been dead much longer
than they'd been alive,
but they were sitting in creaking old rockers
on top of their graves
gossiping about the weather.
They knew by their arthritis,
by their rheumatism,
by their trick knee
that it was bad.
They weren't talking about wind and rain.
Their false teeth can hear the world hurting.
They'd made pies for 4th of July picnics
and voted every year with their husbands
wearing their sunday best,
but this is different.

Deep in their graves
the dirt around their skeletons
tugs and cries like any of their children
up all night with the croup.
Each of the old women has stories
of miracle cures she found
for her own children,
stories the children heard repeated
for at least 40 years. They're dead now too
and don't have to listen anymore.
But this is the world.

The old women rock,
their flowered housedresses clean,
their gnarled fingers nimble enough
to stroke an occasional squirrel.
One of them knits the fog into a wool jacket

in case it gets cold
and because she's used to knitting.
One of them was buried with a bible
but her family forgot her reading glasses
so she keeps it in her handbag,
she was never much of a reader anyway.

Things have been getting worse for a long time.
Ever since Bill and how strange he was
when he got back from the war,
jumping when anyone spoke to him
and staring at ordinary things,
then apologizing with his face all red,
they weren't surprised when it happened.
Sometimes the boy's name changes,
they never say what happened
or even which war.
Or ever since the factory closed;
or ever since the factory opened.

The old women know all the words
to songs no one remembers;
they danced to them once.
They know the smell of coffee
when everyone else is still asleep.
They know what to say to an awkward grandchild
who thinks everyone hates her.
They know many things,
they don't know if it will be enough.
Their trick knee is never wrong.
The old women rocked
and gossiped about the weather.
They weren't talking about wind and rain.

LONELY MACHINES

Machines in closed-down factories are lonely.
They sit unused, not yet allowed to rust
or have pieces stolen
because the factory still exists on paper.
Machines do not feel.
They are lonely the way they are iron and steel.
The only difference between the lonely wire
and the generator
is that the generator is off.
The security guard is paid the same
as he was when the machines growled and hummed
and made whatever they made:
cans, weapons, flashlights, toy trains, etc.
The machines are not lonely
for the men who fed them,
men who stand in unemployment lines,
men who yell at their wives
that it's not their fault,
men who have to look at their children.
Machines have no memory and anyway,
all men are the same.
Machines are cold. They sit.
Only the lonely wire still works,
making loneliness,
and the machines no more question it
than they ever questioned Agent Orange
or souvenir ashtrays from Las Vegas.

VAMPIRES

I know why vampires are so popular.
These days, we're all drained anyway.
Rent goes up, pay goes down,
arguments with lovers and ex-lovers,
reminders of broken promises in the mail
between doctor bills telling you
a new set of tests might be advisable,
a broken toilet and the plumber can't come
till after his son's school play,
traffic jams, expired bus transfers
and the sort of music they play
when they've put your phone call on hold forever.
We're all drained anyway,
we might as well be beautifully drained.
If all the daily details are going to eat our souls
the way termites eat wood, boring thru
without even noticing we're alive
until one day we're dead - well,
vampires aren't boring.
And they never have to lug those marvelous capes
to the laundry
or make humiliating dentist's appointments
to be told they must floss their fangs.
Granted vampires kill their lovers,
but they never disappoint them.
And it takes a long, enchanted weakening time
"the world well lost" so to speak.
Those long, strong fingers,
those pale, predatory smiles.
There are no vampires, but that's a minor objection.
That doesn't stop people from wanting them.
From needing them.
After all, there is no justice
and that doesn't stop people either.

FOR ERIC

I just got a phone call from a friend
who is back in the nut house again
so he's calling collect
and who can refuse collect calls from a nut house?
And of course, it's at the other end of the state.
I ask him if he stopped taking his medication
and he says, offended,
that has nothing to do with it,
he has a mission and he has to go to heaven
but not to worry he'll always be a poet,
how am I?
And there's this magazine he's supposed to be in,
is it out yet?
"No it isn't," I tell him
leaving the rest of his speech alone.
(I used to try to argue but it doesn't help.)
He doesn't sound drugged.
He says he'll be out soon
but it doesn't really matter
he can write anywhere, he has to go now,
he wishes I wouldn't make such a fuss.
O.K. This has all happened before.
But if the long-distance operator rings me
with a collect call from heaven
I'm not accepting the charges.

RAIN ON THE STREET

As wind turns leaves over
so even the undersides get wet
so the street people get soaked inside out,
entrails blowing in the cold
barely connected by a leaf stem
at the base of the spine.
It rains inside our lungs.
It rains inside our brains.
Crumpled cigarette wrappers and used kleenex
float down our overflowing veins.
It rains inside our mouths
and words melt together like wet print.
It rains inside our eyes
colder and older than tears.
It rains inside our already drenched
triple pairs of socks.
Rain pours out of our heads like hair.
    We are raining on the street.
    We are raining on the world.

FOR ROSEBUD AND PEOPLE'S PARK

I've avoided the Park lately.
Even the dirt looks too dirty.
Even the flowers look guilty.
Territorial paranoid little fights.
Sullen charity food.
Piles of lifeless socks.
Maybe People's Park only means something
to people who were there at the beginning;
maybe I should stick to my memories.

But Rosebud was 19 when they shot her;
she wasn't even born
when we made that Park.
She was ready to die for it
and maybe tried to kill for it.
I don't know what that is,
but it sure isn't nostalgia.

What is it with that place?

They said they had to kill Rosebud to stop her;
she died in the chancellor's house
because the chancellor built a volleyball court
on People's Park.

There were swingsets and children once;
but Rosebud never saw them.

The cops roust people with dreary regularity.
Shopping cart madness.

Guys whose ambition in life
is to look like they're on a wanted poster
with a big reward.
Some good music. Many boring speeches
and the sound system never works.

Now there's demonstrations
and a batch of naked people
smeared with mud and leaves
danced in front of the riot police
and everyone's wearing buttons that say
"Long Live Rosebud".
I looked at her picture in the paper.
She was smiling a little.
A guy on the street told me she was a blonde.

She was 19. I don't think I knew her.
I don't think I know anything.

AMERICA

I'm remembering America.
There was such a place once.
A wooden front porch, its paint faded.
A grandfather or an uncle in a rocker
creaking as if the wood had arthritis.
He watches the fat overfleshed roses
drop their petals and he talks like water.
Sometimes the others listen, sometimes not.
It doesn't matter.
The screen door's warped, it won't stay closed
unless it's locked. The children slam it
but never lock it.
The whole house is like that,
full of things that don't quite work.
It doesn't matter.
America is not this comfortable house
with potatoes peeled in the kitchen
and a kitten feverishly weaving around ankles
in case the potatoes magically turn to catfood.
America is this house magically transformed.
It was going to be a skyscraper, a palace,
it was going to be beautiful.
But America is magic
and that should've warned us.
Magic is tricky.
America transformed into kitty litter boxes
and we don't know how it happened.
And we can't even changes our own boxes
and the smell is getting worse.

PORTRAIT OF A GIRL

A girl with blue hair walks down the street
playing with a chinese fan,
snapping it open and shut,
waving it under her chin as she arches her neck.
She looks new as a mushroom
just sprouted after the rain
in spite of fashionably old black silk.
It can't have taken her 18 years to reach 18;
she's been instantly assembled in a factory,
or appeared in a puff of smoke blue as her hair
and was given the chinese fan
to weigh her to earth.
She was never a child
with parents telling her what to do,
nobody ever told her what to do
and her legs have always been long.
Her skin's smooth as the new mushrooms
that are smaller than her breasts
but not by much.
She fans away a blue curl
then taps the closed fan
against the back of her other hand.
It's simple enough:
she knows everything
and was definitely born yesterday.

BIG TRUCKS

The big semi trucks driven by rednecks all night,
cutting off cars full speed,
wheels as tall as a churchdoor,
beating the road into submission,
stopping at truckstops for beer and bad jokes
and always uneasy too far away from their machines,
what are they carrying?
Those big men popping their knuckles,
popping pills to stay up
and sneering at the side effects,
those big trucks,
the terrors of every intersection,
packed tight, piled in back,
roaring right past customs
and giving the finger.
What are they carrying?
Poems. Poems.
All the poems I haven't written yet.

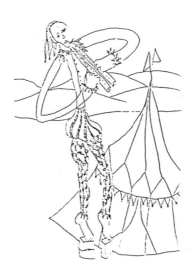

THE NEW DEPRESSION

When things started to go wrong
everyone had scapegoats picked out,
made speeches, got into fights,
felt strong and righteous.
After all, as soon as we got rid of
the rich or the poor, the cops or the robbers,
the blacks or the whites, the young or the old
everything would be all right.
And it was going to be tough
but of course we'd succeed, it was kinda fun.
Like an old cowboy movie.
But things got worse and it goes on and on.
All the names filled with water.
It doesn't even feel good to swear anymore.
It doesn't even feel good to piss anymore.
We wake up tired and walk along
staring at the sidewalk,
sometimes bumping into someone
and snarling without conviction.
Not even looking up
to see if it's someone we don't like.
It really doesn't matter,
we're just not interested.
Everyone's a hurting blur.
The mirror also.
We're finally achieving equality.

SCARECROW

An old scarecrow, black coat torn at the elbows,
old black tophat
stuck in a field of corn
not even the crows believed him.
They tweaked straw from his neck
to line their nests
and the green corn grew and grew.

One night in the dark of the moon
that scarecrow, he climbed down,
walked to the edge of the field
where a limousine waited,
a long black limousine.
He got in, spit one straw into black gloves
and said "Drive". The chauffeur drove
and the green corn grew and grew.

They said bullets wouldn't kill him.
There were stories of men
who emptied machine guns into him
and he just looked bored,
later what was left of them
was thrown to the crows.
They said it wasn't safe
to look at him too close
'cause what you see, it don't make sense.
They said nothing got to him,
no drugs, no women,
he wouldn't even bother to get a new coat,
why should he,
everyone knew who he was
and the green corn grew and grew.

People died.
Money changed hands.
People killed.
Money changed hands.
They were so used to it everyone believed him,
except the crows who sat on his windowsill
cawing all night. Cawing all night.
He stayed up all night to listen.

One night in the dark of the moon
he got back in his limousine,
his long black limousine,
and rode to the field of corn,
walked to the center
and climbed back on his cross.
An old scarecrow, black coat torn at the elbows,
not even the crows believed him.
They pecked out his eyes
and the blood flowed down
and the red corn grew and grew.

FOR POLLY, WHO DIED

Nothing I remember about you
adds up to a death.
I saw you 2 weeks ago at a party.
You looked good, you fake-flirted
for the camera, showing a garter,
36 playing at 16,
we've got the pictures, see?
No.
You were half blind from diabetes
all your life
but that's not why you can't see now.
I remember how pleased you were
when someone called your name on the street.
You got me my place. You helped a lot of people.
You kept an attack-trained respectability
on a leash. It won fights.
You almost died so many times
I stopped believing in your death.
Almost dying was just something you did,
the way other friends got arrested, strung out
or kept breaking up and getting back
with their lovers
and they're still here.
And I still can't believe you're not.
I'm writing this to read at a memorial
and I know I'll be glancing at the door
to see if you've got here yet. Blonde hair,
white dress, glitter on your fingernails,
explaining the people who brought you got lost,
are you very late?
Yes, Polly. Yes, you are.
But look, we waited for you.

FOR RODNEY KING

Because a man was beaten by 4 other men
women singing in the showers
adjust the faucets carefully
between "hot" and "cold" and "blood".
Because a man was beaten by 4 other men
they're selling t-shirts in the ruins:
"welcome to LA, the cops will treat you
like a king".
Because a man was beaten by 4 other men
a finger broke off a famous statue
and a 7 year old boy took it home.
He hid it in a drawer, rolled in a sock.
He took it out at night; it felt so cold.
He pretended it was a gun.
Because a man was beaten by 4 other men
on video
another man was beaten by 4 other men
on video.
So much for video.
Because a man was beaten by 4 other men
psychiatrists say it is dangerous
for children to watch the news
without parental supervision.
Because a man was beaten by 4 other men
the devil was at the crossroads at midnight
and people came to him to *buy* souls,
theirs had worn out.
And worst of all
because a man was beaten by 4 other men
    nothing happened.

19

3 CARD MOLLY

I walked out of my building
and there was a big crowd
around a guy playing 3 card molly.
He had a good rap and worked the crowd
with eyes and arms, he was almost a dancer.
A guy standing a little off
told me the dealer had 3 shills and had made
"at least a hundred in the past half hour".
A trembly old man, unshaven,
who I'd seen stumbling about the street
as if the pavement were quicksand
was trying to push his way closer.
He wanted to gamble the handful of twenties
from his Social Security check.
He was in a great hurry to lose.
He was old enough to've seen 3 card molly
in a dozen different cities
but either he didn't remember
or he didn't care.
The rest of the crowd was shouting, pushing kids,
egging each other on. As if they could win.
The cards slapped down, promising.
The dealer made loud sounds of surprise
as if he can't imagine
why they fell like that.
And just this once
the old man held hot exciting money
as if he could play.
As if he could lose.

DEJA VU

I think I saw then 20 years ago.
I'm sure I saw them 20 years ago.
They're both about 20.
A pretty, long-haired blonde girl
in a black fringed suede jacket
and a flowered dress
who believes in god,
and an eager, idealistic scruffy young guy
who believes in communism
arguing in the outdoor cafe,
obviously in love.
"But just because I can't touch it
doesn't mean I don't believe," she says,
her voice lingering on the world "touch".
"But the objective material world,"
he says in a husky, non objective voice.
Now they're talking about "reality"
as if it were a puppy
they were trying to housebreak
and the girl is playing
with a small blue flower.
It's so simple to both of them
and they'll never convince each other,
and they can't look at each other
without smiling.
Will I see them again, still 20
in another 20 years?

AFTER A STREET RIOT

I've been looking at my reflection
in broken shop windows
each time different:
whether a pattern of cracks
around a bullet hole covers my face
like a church veil,
or pieces of the glass fell out
along with sections of me,
leaving my reflection
an incomplete cubist jigsaw puzzle.
I've been looking, comparing,
who am I afterwards?
The glass bleeds,
I touch my uncut face.
This was the very best businesslike
guaranteed unbreakable plasticglass.
It wasn't good enough.
It had no defense against a rage
already broken and howling.
I don't know where I belong in all this
but I take my face
from one broken shop window to the next.
These are the only mirrors
I can believe.

FLY AGAINST A WINDOWPANE

I am a fly beating my wings
against solid air that will not let me thru.
Outside the screams, the blood and fire.
Poets and flies are drawn to wounds.
I beat the air and bruise my wings.
If I keep this up flies will feed on me
and understand. That is how things are.
When I was human I played King of the Castle
with my cousins in twilight.
The coming night rose from the ground
dragging damply at our ankles.
There was a grey slab where hills became forest.
I don't remember anyone reaching it.
I don't remember my cousins' faces.
I think they had none. Only shouts.
When I skinned my knee it hurt:
blood where the rock scraped
and dirt where I slid down. There was no crown,
no prize. None was needed.
Why don't my wings work?

Night does not fall. It rises from the earth;
it has reached my knees.
Armies play King of the Castle
with clumsy tanks and clumsier bodies.
It's Sunday afternoon in the trenches,
the flies praise God
and God receives their prayers.
I am a poet. I cannot even weep.
If I arranged plastic orange cones
that mark highway accidents
around the human heart no one would stop.
I have seen the end of the world
pictured in smoke from a young girl's cigarette

23

while wind blew fine hairs like foam on her arm.
I saw a blur, puzzled at being over.
And then over.
But she was more worth watching
than the vision. People are.
She had new hoop earrings
and swung them for her friends.
Back and forth. Back and forth.
Poets and flies are drawn to wounds.

Tomorrow the coffee shop where I write this
will be razed. I touch the table top
pretending to be marble as I pretend to touch.
A woman loaded down with laundry
(white sheets against her heavy hair)
passes me on the narrow staircase.
We both look guiltily away
as if we knew where the bodies were buried.
We do.
They're still alive but that doesn't matter.
Enough have died. We know that too.
We say nothing.
She's lived here 5 years.
We have not learned each other's names.
If I were human would I have a name?
And would the flies come when I died?

NUT ON THE STREET

He's just a nut on the street
spouting off the usual.
But then I notice he's recording it all
into a baby tape
"and this is life on the street, part 2,"
he says, turning the tape over.
Then he makes a gun motion with thumb
and forefinger to execute the machine.
"Bang," he says. And giggles.
The nut has a circle of small objects
carefully arranged in front of him:
a rubber band, a cigarette butt,
a piece of wadded tissue, a stone.
He squats down and tells stories with them,
making them ambush each other,
he's getting even with all of them.
The nut's about 32, thin and has a soft gleeful
I-told-you-so voice.
Often enough I miss the words.
No, not often enough.
And the recorder doesn't miss a thing.
When the nut walks off abruptly
the circle of small objects looks at me
accusingly.
They want to know how the story comes out.
I don't want to tell them
they all die in the end,
even the nut who set them up couldn't tell them.
And I don't want anyone to see me talking
to a small circle of objects on the street;
I don't even have a tape recorder.
I walk off, abruptly.

HAIR WRAP

I'm watching a couple at the hair wrap carpet
on the street having bright threads braided
in the hair at the back of their necks
for a small donation. It's not easy.
For one thing, he doesn't *have* any hair
at the back of his neck
but the people at the stand are resourceful.
Red, green, blue, yellow.
The couple looks solemn
as if they were having their love tied on
so they wouldn't lose it.
Orange, brown, purple.
She holds her long curly blonde hair
away from her neck, her head down by her knees
so they can work behind her, fingers dancing.
He doesn't look at her.
They're very young.
I read of a sea captain once
who always went to a weather witch
before he set sail.
She'd braid the winds up for him
for a small donation.
The winds are rising now.
Red, green, yellow, blue.
And the thunder.
Orange, brown, purple.

26

BOY LOOKING OUT THE BUS WINDOW

A small boy looks out the bus window
excited by houses going by
as if they were toys meant to be played with,
arranged, knocked over, the church
balanced on its steeple just to see
if it will fall down.
A gas station with bright red pumps
will almost fit into the boy's hand.
He reaches for it, palm flat on the window.
He breathes on the glass, climbing over his mother,
grabbing at traffic lights as they swoop by
like butterflies.
She tells him sit down, behave, be good,
play with the plastic ninja turtles
she brought for him, be quiet.
A necklace of buzzing negatives she always wears,
a little under a locket
with an embarrassing baby picture in it.
He doesn't listen.
A girl with pink framed glasses reads a romance novel.
A man reads yesterday's newspaper as if he cared.
A group of teenage jackets
finish each other's sentences, they laugh a lot.
Old women stare straight ahead, laundering memory
like a drug dealer launders money.
A businessman checks his watch.
Only the boy looks out the bus window
but not at the world.
He's too young for distance and perspective
so he's looking at toys.
His toys.
Better than his ninja turtles.
Houses and people belong to him;
he's going to play with them.

STREET SKETCH

"Why do you have so many dogs?"
a tourist asked a street dude
who was standing firmly astride squirming leashes,
his hat at a jaunty angle, ready to ride the air.
"Because," the street dude answered,
"this one's a *man*" (and he looked his questioner
up and down, mocking the expensive clothes)
"and this one's a girl and some day
I'll have 20 dogs behind me,
20 dogs in front of me and 10 to each side.
Yeah"
He turned away as if the tourist
had ceased to exist
and leaned down to scratch an ear.
"Yeah," he repeated softly
already thinking about something else.
But just for a second I saw it,
the whole shaggy tribe of them,
only the dangling cigarette
marking out the human.
Eyes gleaming. Wagging their tails.
Howling at the moon.

WARNING

Last night was friday when young guys
stand on street corners
and try to stare down the cops,
cruising the girls,
aiming a cigarette like a machinegun
and daring the world to look at them funny.
Like any friday night.
Except last night they threw bottles,
broke windows, yelled, lit fires in the street.
A comic book store was looted.
A bartender got his head broken
when he stuck it out to see what the hell.
No politics, not remotely.
No indignant protest flyers
giving directions and begging people to turn up.
No warning and only police blockades
eventually turned people away
along with cars and buses.
This has been happening a lot on weekends
instead of parties, movies or nightclubs.
Instead of places where people wear expensive clothes
or where they charge at the door.
The price of bread goes up every 2 weeks
at the market.
Everyone can afford a stone.

SATURDAY NIGHT

It's a hot saturday night.
I came up to my room but I can't get away.
There's a nightclub with a terrible band
sweating under my arm.
There's a tribe of sparechangers
with their palms out
standing on my palm.
They want. I want. It's hot.
The BART train rides under my hair
where I used to part it
when I wore it in braids.
Long ago.
There's a pair of lovers
having an intimate talk
in the secluded restaurant booth of my ear
where no one will eavesdrop but me.
Their voices tremble.
There's a barker with red suspenders
and a Bogart hat
leaning in front of my belly button
as if there were a strip joint inside.
He's not telling the truth
but he tells it very well.
There's a corner liquor store
in the crook of my elbow,
a crossroads of bones and bums.
The dead come here to buy beer.
I recognize some of them.
It's too hot for them to sleep.
And it's saturday night.
A biker gang speeds up and down my back;
I'm rather sorry, I'd like to watch.
Drawled laughing curses.
I'm in my room, my door's locked,

my windows are shut
but the city pours thru the crack
under the door
drowning the dark.
The one way streets cover my body
like a plaid skin full of trucks,
cop cars, and cabbies telling drunks
"yeah,
I'll tell you where the girls are."
There's even a Holiday Inn on my shoulder
where tourists look at the view
and raise their cameras.
They're not taking pictures of my room,
at least I hope not.
There is no city,
there is no heat,
there is no saturday night.
Or so I tell myself.
But I can't get away.

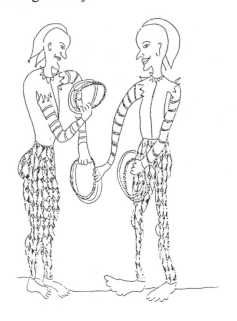

31

THE LATEST BUTTON

I saw a guy wearing a button
with a knife and fork on it.
Underneath it said:
"Will be President for food".
I can't think of a better reason
to be president,
though that's a long time
to wait for a meal.
Politics and economics
are just boom-boom words.
Numbers are a conspiracy
to make everyone go away.
I told the guy I'd vote for him
and asked about the button.
He had bad teeth and freckles.
"Yeah," he told me,
"the Will Work for Food signs
don't work anymore.
First, there isn't any work
and second, guys on waiting lists
get mad at us, as if we were going to steal
the jobs they're not going to get either.
This way people just laugh."
He shrugged. He was too skinny
to be that cheerful.
    There aren't any jobs.
    There isn't any food.

THE DARK

I'm afraid of the dark.
I used to be scared just before I fell asleep
and then I'd wake up in the morning.
But the dark has been changing;
it doesn't just come out at night anymore.
I se it at brightly lit parties
where everyone's drinking too much
and laughing too much
and trying not to look at the dark.
I see it at high noon. Businessmen
on their lunch hour are afraid of the dark,
they walk fast but they're too scared to run
and there's nowhere to run to.
Everything that can be controlled
is under control. It's not enough.
I've seen the dark steal coins
from sparechangers, to wear on its eyes.
I've watched the dark rise in the morning,
like the sun. I've heard the dark
uncoiling from the tongues of quarreling lovers
who used to love the dark.
When I get home my answering machine
is blinking but there's no message.
That was the dark who called. I know.
I'm scared. I used to see the dark
just before I fell asleep at night.
But I sleep less and less now
and I see the dark everywhere.

STREET SAXOPHONE

It's not even a separate sound.
It gets walked like a drunk's puppy
yapping and tangling the cords
as the song stumbles and catches itself
and the bottle, and takes another drink.
A street saxophone with its brass hole
as empty and full as a sparechanger's hand,
blood and grime and music in the way
floating down the gutter
with orange peels and cigarette butts.
Music absorbed into the walls like graffiti.
Music road-killed by each passing car
and resurrected.
The guy playing the saxophone
doesn't go in for being visible,
he's busy.
The doorway ate most of him anyway,
long ago.
Only lips and fingers left
and the sounds
we call a street
and walk on.

STREET SKETCH

He had one arm in a tie-dye shirt sling
and told me he was Robin Hook
and looked at my poetry
and started to read one out loud to some girl
and said it was his poem.
I said it was not either
and he laughed at me.
"Ooooh, you're *so* possessive," he said.
"I was Asmodeus Mozart in a past life,
I don't own anything, maybe we're soul mates,
maybe we both own it.
Didja ever think of that? Huh?"
Well no.
Not that poem.
Maybe this one.

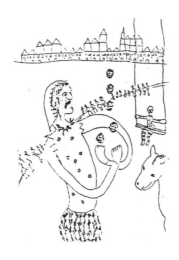

BOSNIA

"You've got to stop this," my head tells me.
"Whaddaya mean, me?" I bluster.
"Go get yourself a hero or something,
join the movies where wars work out right,
go organize a whole batch of people,
other people,
go away and leave me alone."
"Ethnic cleansing.
Concentration camps.
You promised," my head tells me.
The only thing worse than a Jewish mother
is a Jewish mother.
"She's dead," my head tells me, "I'm you."
"You're not helping," I answer.
"Neither are you and you *promised*,"
my head reminds me again.

I put my hands in my ears
but it goes on talking.
"Forget politics,
if the bombs start falling
it's all right, I won't bug you."
"Thanks a lot," I mutter sarcastically.
"You'll be dead of course,"
my head continues calmly
"but so will everyone else
so it won't matter;
you won't have broken any promises.
Holocaust. Ethnic cleansing.
Or are you going to claim you don't remember?"

I try reason,
something I only do

when I know I'm going to lose anyway.
"Look," I say, "these are prison camps,
there's talk about death camps
but no proof.
They compare everything to Hitler,
I think he makes them feel real,
and it's a civil war, suppose both sides
are running death camps?
And just how am I supposed to stop all this
anyway?"

My head doesn't even bother
with such mundane details.
"You promised," it repeats again.
"You know you promised."
There isn't really anything to say.
"Yeah," I admit.
"I know."

PUPPIES ON THE STREET

A big brown dog with 6 new puppies,
tired teats drooping.
She sways like a broken backed horse
and she wants to sleep,
she pushes the puppies away
as they come nuzzling: 2 light brown,
2 dark brown, 1 black,
and 1 black with white paws.
None of them will stay in the cardboard box
where their owner put them
on top of each other.
The box is too small
and the bottom's about to give way.
The puppies' teeth are soft,
they bite each other's faces
and wag their feet off balance.
They don't really look like dogs yet,
they look like furry muffins with paws.
Passersby question their owner
but they don't look at her.
She has a faded bedroll and dogfood
and I think she lives on the street.
She looks as tired
as if she'd just had puppies herself.
She must keep them till they're weaned.
Then she breaks off to chase the black one
which stumbles off the curb
into the path of the car.
She catches it out of harm's way
and croons.
Who will catch her?

FOR PETER, WHO DIED

I write your death poem on April Fool's Day
because your life was a joke
and you wanted it like that.
Your body was twisted as a cartoon
so you twisted your tongue to match,
if I'd seen word balloons over your head
I wouldn't have been surprised.
You twisted your mind with as much work
as you could've used training it.
You were fascinated with phone numbers,
I remember yours spelled orgy-something
and everyone forgot the something.
You taught me to dial "popcorn" for the time,
I still taste butter and salt when I call it.
You talked like a hormone-crazed turnip
but you knew every cultural event
and went to as many as you scored rides to.
There was a woman you never let yourself love,
there was a son you never got to know,
but there was enough strungout jailbait
who'd trade sex for drugs
so if you were lonely you didn't have to notice.
You were determined to be useless.
To live indigestibly inside a bellylaugh.
You succeeded.
Near the end you fought with everyone
over nonsense, and nonsense wasn't fun anymore.
When you strung out some of my friends
I stopped saying "Oh well, it's only Peter".
But I'll say it now. As an epitaph?
As a joke? I'm sorry, Peter.
You got what you wanted.
April Fool.

HAPPINESS

Happiness always feels like a mistake.
It rarely happens when planned for.
On "happy occasions" everyone's too nervous
and too sure something will go wrong.
A burp. A cough. A blown tire.
Birthdays. Even weddings can't be enjoyed
until they're over. Happiness is more
like going thru the morning's bills
and finding a draft notice to the war in heaven
and a box with a pair of wings inside.
The whole thing disappears at a touch,
it was a wrong address
but those alien feathers felt so warm.
You look at your hand
not even aware you're smiling.
Or the way the light falls sometimes
till you're afraid someone will come
take away your eyes,
you're not supposed to see this.
Or singing loudly off key, half crying
and totally drunk in a bar
loving everyone for about a minute and a half.
There's a fight later in an attempt to prove
you're still human when the happiness is gone.
It only works as a distraction.
Winning and love and money are very good
but they're part of our world
and we can claim to understand them.
Happiness is dust
left over from the original creation,
dancing dust unchanged by time.
It blows in our faces for no reason
and for no reason, blows away.

L.A. BURNING

I'm not going to describe those fires.
I don't have a t.v., I didn't see them
in a square box with a suit and tie
interviewing the burning buildings.
I grew up in Pasadena,
I wanted to burn it down myself,
long ago, for my own reasons.
I was somewhere else at the time,
I can prove it. I have nothing to say
and the fires say it for me.
It's too easy to write about injustice;
everyone's against it.
It's too hard to write about injustice
as if you gave a damn
outside the poem.
I never saw the videotape
because I don't have a t.v.
Maybe someday I will stop seeing the videotape.
Maybe not.
All I ever knew about the Watts riots
was a picture book of the Watts towers.
I didn't see those fires either.
I didn't set those fires either.
The radio tells me everything is under control.
Or almost under control.
Or will be under control
very soon.
Don't they know the core of the earth is fire?
No fireman can put it out.
And I was somewhere else at the time;
I can prove it.

STREET PORTRAIT

He walks as if his arms and legs
weren't quite connected to his body.
He talks as if his tongue
wasn't quite connected to his throat.
He smiles in a twitchy way,
he twitches in a smiley way
and sometimes he won't go away.
He turns up with his head shaved occasionally,
"Lice," he says proudly.
He wears a flappy dark coat,
the kind farmers put on a scarecrow
and his wristbones look
as if the meat's been eaten off them.
He likes to have his picture taken.

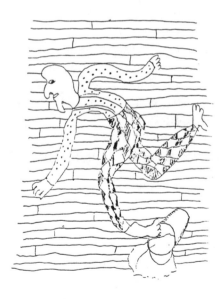

MURAL

More and more, the world reminds me of a mural,
a tropical island painted on the wall
of a warehouse next to a junkyard
in the middle of the projects.
As long as I look at the surface
I'm supposed to look at everything's all right.
An inch to one side fuck-off graffiti
claims territory and threatens instant death.
The worse the neighborhood
the brighter the parrots
and rainbows in the mural,
the riper the piles of painted fruit
so close to the charity soup line.
The more drive-by shootings
the more loving the descriptions of heaven
feather by feather in the angel's wings;
this world doesn't work anymore, trade it in.
The happy people I see outside
are on murals or huge advertising billboards
making love to cigarettes.
The happy people I see inside are on t.v.
And by now I don't really believe anything.
Didn't we use to be people?
Didn't people use to be us?
The sun's out today and the new leaves,
everyone's strolling and it *looks* nice.
But is it just painted on?
Is there nothing behind it
but damp rotting plaster
and a child with a bad cough
who wants a glass of water?

BOY ON A SKATEBOARD

Wind blows his ribs like ripples
as he stretches around cars.
Rubberband boy on a skateboard
tall as a wheel on a big truck
that's much too close to his left elbow.
His speed isn't miles per hour,
it's what he's getting away with,
what he's leaving behind.
His old tennis shoes shake off
a yellow schoolbus and all the armheld,
namestamped books.
The skateboard runs over years of homework,
the late nights jumped like curbs.
He leaves behind nations
stretching dying hands after him
out of a blown newspaper 2 days out of date
and rolling down the sidewalk
like urban tumbleweed.
And he's not riding into the future.
The jobs he'll hold, wife, family, station wagon,
a divorce, a bar, some shadow friends
a little too good at pool -
all these belong to a boy
who never rode a skateboard.
He has no name now. Faded shorts.
Holding a smile between his teeth
the way an otter holds a fish
that still might get away.
He leaves himself behind
and doesn't notice.

FIDDLER ON THE STREET

Fiddle tucked under his chin
as he frowns down on it.
Sawing away wildly, making it wail,
stomping in time. Corn liquor mountain music
from places where people
are an endangered species
no one wants to protect.
16 maybe, attempting an unconvincing mustache.
Curly hair. Fighting the fiddle
with every muscle in his arms.
He could be good looking if it occurred to him.
It won't.
There should be boulders,
the entrance to a used up coal mine
and a hollow tree behind him.
But he's playing on the street
in front of a shoe store
with high-heeled purple boots in the window.
He's barefoot.
The crowd on the street goes from impressed
to confused. "Wild" to them means sexy.
This is older.
A fist clenching the sky.
Blackberries in a bruised mouth.
Fiddle and the moon, maybe a screech owl.
No one else around.

WHERE I GREW UP

Grandfather's bookcase went nearly
up to the ceiling
with a glass front over the books
and a key in the candy dish
on top of the bookcase.
I used to climb on the back of a chair
to steal the key at night.
The pages of many books had never been cut,
it was like raping virgins.
I read with a knife in one hand
and a flashlight in the other,
I was supposed to be asleep.
It was a quiet house.
The air-conditioner absorbed the t.v.
The always vacuumed blue carpet covered our throats.
Mother tended African violets
on the kitchen ledge
but there was always something wrong with them.
Always. Always.
Always lived in that house more than we did
and I was always too young to understand.
We had a Ming lamp in the shape of a horse
and I thought Ming was the horse's name.
Mother brushed her hair a hundred times
at a blue glass vanity table
with an oval mirror
and put it up with tortoiseshell combs.
Father went to work.
I talked to the people in books.
I talked to Ming
and planned to ride him away.
Always sat on all the chairs so softly.
Nobody lived in that house.

TOO MANY DEATHS

There are too many deaths.
I'm sick of describing people
who aren't there
as if I could send a wanted poster
to the world of the dead
with approximate portraits,
just what could I offer as a reward?
I used to believe
in waking up their memories every morning
and washing where their faces used to be,
ice cold water to shock their eyes open.
I used to repeat
the way a forefinger would tap a wrist
or the way hair at the back of a neck
would never behave.
I'd drag their images
through familiar motions.
But there are too many dead
and I've been talking to them
almost exclusively.
I can't tell them
what it's like to be alive;
I don't think I know anymore.

BLUES

Don't tell me to grow up;
I'm so sad I'm gonna throw up.
Dead birds don't sing so good.
Here comes the blues
and there goes the neighborhood.
Some doors don't open to kisses.
I heard about the last chance dance
but I didn't go. Did you?
I've got the amalgamated suicide piano blues
and I think your familiar just ate my shoes.
If it were raining
I could blame the rain.
Little baby girl dressed in Daddy's pink slips
from a dozen lost jobs blues.
I've got the blues.

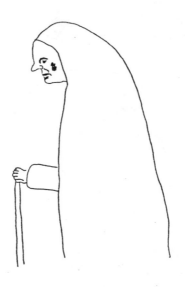

DIRECTIONS FOR A FRIEND VISITING RUSSIA
(for Bruce)

When you see my brothers,
when you see my sisters,
when you see my enemies,
when you see my lovers,
ask, ask,
ask what the weather's like
after the end of the world,
inside private tents of women's hair
let down heavily as garage doors,
inside public again churches unused so long
the darkness creaks, in line for food,
for word of mouth. Do children play hopscotch
on the old stone streets?
Tell me the real news;
tell me the jumprope counting songs
with clattering heels.
Tell me the color of a kitchen wooden chair.
Are toilets broken, are hearts broken?
And what is spoken
now that only speech is free?

When you see my brothers,
when you see my sisters,
when you see my enemies,
when you see my lovers,
ask, ask,
ask about the war between ghosts and statues.
Ask the names of wildflowers
too common for names.
Ask for water when you wake at night, thirsty.
Are there many jobs available
re-writing history textbooks,
feeling armies dribble thru your fingers

and old yellow documents twisting like smoke?
Go to the Kremlin, does it still look
like a hot fudge sundae?
Swirling, rich, forbidden?
Go to the hospital to visit Time;
tell me what he tells you,
but don't tell me to believe it.
Throw a pebble in the river and say my name
and I'll hear water and rotting leaves.

When you see my brothers,
when you see my sisters,
when you see my enemies,
when you see my lovers,
ask, ask,
ask for directions and see where they think
you want to go.
Ask for a cup of coffee thick as licorice.
Ask one of the old men
playing chess in the park
what year it is.
Ask him what went wrong, where it hurts
and can you see pictures
of his grandchildren?
Ask the wind, is it a good day?
Ask what they see,
when they look at you.

Julia Vinograd is a Berkeley street poet. She has published 34 books of poetry, and won the American Book Award of The Before Columbus Foundation. She received a B.A. from the University of California at Berkeley and an M.F.A. from the University of Iowa.

Other titles from Zeitgeist Press:

Graffiti by Julia Vinograd $4.95
Bad Dog Blues by Bruce Isaacson $4.95
Imaginary Conversation With Jack Kerouac
by Jack Micheline $5.00
I Want A New Gun by David Lerner $4.95
Compass In An Armored Car by Bana Witt $4.95
The Animals We Keep in the City by Eli Coppola $4.95
Horn Of Empty by Julia Vinograd $4.95
The Cities Of Madame Curie by Laura Conway $4.95
American Romance by Eliot Schain $3.00
On This Train by Tommy Swerdlow $3.00
Going For The Low Blow by Vampyre Mike Kassel $3.00
Street Samurai by Julia Vinograd $4.95
Where's My Wife by Jennifer Blowdryer $3.00
The Wino, The Junky, and the Lord
by Kathleen Wood $5.00
The Underclassified by Julia Vinograd $4.95
Why Rimbaud Went To Africa by David Lerner $5.95
Evil Spirits And Their Secretaries by David West $5.00
As For Us by David Gollub $5.00
love affairs with barely any people in them
by Bruce Isaacson $5.95
Suspicious Characters by Julia Vinograd $4.95
BAR by David West $3.00
the beat years by Dave Gerard $3.00
Dogs In Lingerie by Danielle Willis $5.95
My Body Is A War Toy by Joie Cook $3.00
Tenderloin Rose by Kathleen Wood $3.00
I Want To Kill Everything by Vampyre Mike Kassel $3.00
In Hotel Rooms Off Broadway by Joanna Spencer $3.00
When There's No More Room In Heck
The Damned Will Walk The Earth by Chris Trian $3.00
The Blind Man's Peep Show by Julia Vinograd $4.95
The Satin Arcane by Jack Hirschman $3.00
Eye Contact Is A Confession by Julia Vinograd $4.95
Wild Kingdom by Vampyre Mike Kassel $3.00
Against the Wall by Julia Vinograd $4.95
Pray Like the Hunted by David Lerner $6.00
The Hummingbird Graveyard by Maura O'Connor $3.00
Special Effects by David Gollub $3.00

Zeitgeist Press
4368 Piedmont Avenue
Oakland, CA 94611 U.S.A.
please add $1 per book for handling and postage